HOW T[O]
Sanity ON A CRACKER

Mom-to-mom whines,
cheese, rants
and recipes

BY JACKIE
HENNESSEY

ISBN: 0985031808
ISBN-13: 9780985031800
LCCN: 2012900656
Jackie Hennessey, Barrington, Rhode Island

This book is dedicated to my husband, Michael.
Without you, this book would still be stuck inside my head.

TABLE OF VENTINGS

Jackie's Pre-Whine and Cheese Venting.

HOW TO SPREAD SANITY ON A CRACKER

Mom-to-mom whines, cheese, rants, and recipes

BY JACKIE HENNESSEY

Like chips without cheese dip, midlife mommy moments wouldn't be the same if we couldn't vent together.

Like many mothers, I have my days. Some you'll find me dusting every corner of my house and baking cookies while hosting a nine-kids-under-age-nine mega playdate. Others, I can barely garner the energy to make my kids' lunches, cancel conference calls, and consume a gossip magazine in one sitting.

Some women never complain or compulsively eat refined sugar or carbohydrates. They never need breaks from their husband or kids. And they could probably live without cheese as long as they live. Bless their hearts, because I'm not one of them. There are afternoons when I have so much on my metaphorical plate, I hide in the pantry, stick a spoon inside a jar of peanut butter, sprinkle some chocolate chips on top, and call it lunch. My mood wavers from manufactured anger to euphoria once a month, every month, to my husband's dismay. It's especially during these times that, regardless of how bloated I get, the only thing that brings me back to normal is whining and eating cheese dip with girlfriends. It's like free therapy. I'm not looking for anyone to solve my problems. I don't need to dissect my past. I simply need to vent. To whine. To let off some steam. There is something so satisfying knowing that other women go through some of the same crap I do. When you realize someone else has to deal with a whiny child in the grocery aisle after four hours of sleep, it's like you won a complimentary manicure, pedicure, and highlights. I realize there are some women who appear to have no problems, no issues, no need to whine or vent. And they probably don't tolerate cheese. At first glance, they may appear normal. They're the easygoing, anxiety-free mothers with babies who sleep through the night, take their first step at ten months and pee in the potty on their second birthday. I envy and despise them simultaneously. I guess I could learn a thing or two from them as well. But maybe I can teach them something, too. That the complaints and problems may vary from woman to woman, but the bottom line remains the same. Look beyond the varied boot labels, bob lengths and bra sizes, and you'll find that we're not so different. Even the most seemingly by-the-baby-book perfect mothers (and even those with frazzled three-year-olds who aren't potty trained,) can use a little time away. Time to whine. Time to vent. Time to let it out. Nothing crazy, just some time away with the girls.

I thoroughly enjoy venting with my girlfriends. Five minutes on the phone is good, but nothing beats a three-hour in-person venting session where you can swap stories over cheese dip. Some people hang glide, backpack through Europe, or sculpt pottery to relieve stress. I like to whine over cheese.

Cheese, A Staple to Any Girls' Night In
(even solo, after a 3 a.m. feeding)

Why cheese? If I could get away with it, I'd eat a brick of cheese every day, about the size of a small car battery. Baked brie, queso dip, goat cheese, you name it, I'd find a way to subsist on it. There is something about cheese. Just the thought of it carries me to a place where I can sit on my rear after putting the kids (and my husband) to bed and watch reruns of my favorite TV shows, pretending the characters are my friends. I can't tell you how many times cheese was present when I vented alone, and with friends. It's an easy-to-fix comfort food, a fundamental part of any girls' night in. When we get together, all you can see are calorie-filled plates with stinky dips, chunky wedges, and overflowing, melting mounds of the stuff. If consumed daily, each would have the power to transform an innocent mother's upper thighs into a set of truck tires. But that is exactly the point. We are busy women—so we don't get together as often as we should. So it's worth it to add a dip or two as we whine and unwind.

I'm not the type to throw formal dinner parties with lavish main courses. I'm more the hors d'oeuvres and desserts girl. Hand me berries, goat cheese, and a sleeve of water crackers and I can turn it into a swanky party platter before you can say "mommy time."

Like most get-togethers, along with cheese comes a fine whine. Whines, ventings, gripes, complaints. Regardless of what you call them, they come with motherhood. And when we hear about other mothers' rants, they trigger something inside us that peels away motherhood-induced stress. As my grandmother once said, motherhood is a lifetime sentence. It's not that it's all bad, but when you become a mother, it can be overwhelming. You think it'll get better by the time your kids get out of diapers. But any physical exhaustion caused by being a new mother turns into emotional exhaustion. Wait for it. And then the tears, tantrums, and inevitable tween years. The challenges never cease, and yes, the rewards are great. Thankfully, there's always whine and cheese. This book combines a chunk of my own personal whines and cheese recipes, along with a collection of real stories from mothers across the country. (From Worcester to Washington.) Thank you all so much for your contributions, ladies! Please note this book is not intended to be a "How To Be a Perfect Mother" guide. Think of it as cheap therapy. My attempt to spread sanity on a cracker. Quick mommy ventings and reflections mixed with cheese dish recipes. These chapters, or ventings, are intended to be brief, because they are based on real mommy time.

To respect the privacy of many of the women who contributed, I changed their names. (Except mine, of course. When you see Jackie, that's me.) Although I wanted to give stripper names, at the last minute I decided it would be in poor taste. So I held back. For those women who asked me to keep their names, whether "Sugar" or "Bambi," God bless, they are untouched.

Whines AND Cheese

VENTING 1

BAKED BRIE AND ONE CRANKY MOM

CHEESE: BAKED BRIE from Shannon in Connecticut

One cheese you can count on at every gathering: baked brie. I must have received a dozen different variations of the same recipe. Because I'm a sucker for a woman with a busy schedule, I picked an easy recipe to accompany the first whine.

> *1 Pie Crust*
> *2 Egg whites*
> *One (8 ounce) wedge of brie*
> *Strawberry Jam*
> *Crackers*

1.) Start with a *ready-made* sheet of pie crust (because everything is better with pie crust). Defrost, wipe with egg whites (this just makes it look fancy and crispy.)

2.) Take one wedge (8 ounces) of your favorite brie and chop it up into pieces.

3.) Make a giant "sack" by placing the cheese on the sheet of pie crust and wrapping it up. The cheese gets gooey and oozes out of the top when it's baked. (Bake at 400 degrees for 15 to 20 minutes.)

4.) You can also get creative and add blackberry or strawberry jam, any type of fruit preserve, nuts, dates, cranraisins, whatever you like with cheese.

5.) Lastly—jazz up the presentation with some fancy or unique crackers (sweet and salty variety) and allow guests to *dive in. So good*—absolute comfort food in a pretty presentation.

WHINE: three thousand miles later, from Jackie

After quitting our jobs, moving from Seattle to Rhode Island, and camping out at my mother-in-law's house until we bought a house of our own, my husband and I found out we were pregnant with our second child. Before thinking our rash decision to move closer to relatives was turning our lives into an after-school-special-gone-to-DVD, it didn't take long for us to land on our feet. We finally settled down in a house on a tree-lined street in Barrington, a suburb a few miles from Providence. My husband found a good job and we were all smiles with our toddler son. For a few weeks. Then the frequent visits from friends and relatives stopped happening so frequently. By the middle of my first trimester, it dawned on me that I was not going back to my job in Seattle. And it left a sinking feeling in my gut, like a prenatal vitamin on an empty stomach. I was blasé and downright cranky. Cranky about leaving my dream job, cranky about the fact that it was twenty degrees colder outside, and cranky that my son was in his terrible twos.

So my husband comes home from work one day, and I start going off. I start picking a fight for no reason. After a week of being Miss Negative Nancy, he snaps. Mind you, my husband is caring and supportive. The man enjoys folding his own laundry, for crying out loud. But he had *had* it with my bitching. Then he says something to me that later inspired me to write this book.

"Babe, I love you, but I don't have a vagina. I think what you need is a night out with the girls."

I consumed a block of cheddar over the next twelve hours. I was livid. Not just because I knew he was right, but because I had just realized I really didn't have anyone to vent to anymore. My closest girlfriends were three thousand miles away, and I was by nature a social butterfly. But it was exhausting enough to fit in a decent shower every day, let alone try to make friends in a new town. I would escape to my mother-in-law's, but I never sat down long enough to share my sob story because my toddler was running around like a maniac and I didn't want to look like I didn't know what I was doing. (Even though I didn't know what I was doing.) I had joined mommy groups, but I was new in town, and what was I going to do, introduce myself, "Hi, my name is Jackie, and if my two-and-a-half-year-old isn't potty trained by next week, I'm sending him to military day camp"?

Unlike women who are embraced by a cul-de-sac of mothers who bake a dozen organic muffins on command, I had rolled my pregnant self into a ball of pitiful, emotional, and hormonal turmoil. In two and a half years, I had moved as far away from Seattle as you can get without leaving the United States and I had gone from bar-hopping with co-workers on Friday nights to waiting in the check-out line to buy a case of pull-ups. And this was considered a night out.

VENTING 2

HOT POPPER AND SOME HEATED MAMAS

CHEESE: HOT POPPER SPREAD from Rosie in Texas

2 (8-ounce) packages of cream cheese, softened
1 cup of mayonnaise
1 can of chopped green chilies, drained
1 (4-ounce) can of diced jalapeno peppers, drained (can also use two 2-ounce cans)
1 cup of grated parmesan cheese

In a large bowl, stir together cream cheese and mayonnaise until smooth. Stir in green chilies and peppers. Pour mixture into a microwave-safe serving dish and sprinkle with parmesan cheese. Microwave on high for about 3 minutes, until the mixture is hot. You could brown the cheese instead — bake at 375°F for 30 minutes.

WHINES: from Rhode Island area moms, bringing what I like to call thirty seconds of sanity

Danielle: My moment of motherhood hell: My husband was away on business. I was at home taking care of our fifteen-month-old and had morning sickness that struck any time of the day. To make matters worse, my son had a stomach virus. Every time I'd change a runny diaper, it made me physically ill. I'd change him on the floor and run to the toilet, change a diaper and run to throw up. This went on for an entire day and night. I thought I'd die!

Caty: My worst mommy moment: My daughter was a few months old when I accidentally nodded off during feeding time. When I woke up, she was on the floor sleeping. I was mortified. She is six now and completely fine. Thankfully, babies are resilient.

Jackie: I was having one of "those" days with my then-three-year-old son. I wanted to do the dishes, he wanted to draw on the kitchen wall. I wanted to fold the laundry, he wanted to dismantle the toilet paper holder and wrap the hallway. I wanted to host a playdate, but he would rather throw himself on the floor and have a tantrum. I tried for two hours off and on to give him a nap, but he refused. When 6 p.m. rolled around, I couldn't take it anymore. As soon as my husband came home, I sighed loudly, handed him to my husband, and went out to buy bread. I came back to find him nestled on my husband's lap fast asleep.

3

VENTING

GET THE CHILI CHEESE CHIP OFF YOUR SHOULDER

CHEESE: CREAMY CHILI CHEESE DIP from Meghan in California

> *1 (8-ounce) package of cream cheese (low fat)*
> *1 can of turkey chili without beans*
> *Hot sauce (1 to 4 teaspoons)*
> *Tortilla chips*

In a saucepan, drop in cream cheese and break it up so it starts to melt. Add homemade chili or a can of chili and mix together until blended. Add hot sauce to your liking. Dip with tortilla chips. Voila!

WHINE: oh, snap, part 1, from Jackie

I'm a mom and a wife. I've been working from home as a public relations consultant for several years, and I often struggle with my role as a stay-at-home-work-from-home mom. I'm like a walking contradiction. When I meet other stay-at-home moms, I feel I need to justify the time I'm working. And when I talk to moms who work out of the house full time, I try relentlessly to justify my non-billable time. Either way, I come across as something I'm really not. Truthfully, what I do works for me. I adore my children and enjoy my work. This is how I see it: Without my children, my life would be empty. And without my work, I would slowly go insane. I'd snap, frankly.

As mothers, we know what it's like to love something unconditionally. Many know what it's like to experience childbirth—to carry and, after forty weeks, push something the size of a large honeydew melon from our unmentionables. It's an incredible, life-changing, mind-altering experience. Before you know it, the nurse sends you home with your little one, and you're donning a mattress-sized maxi pad over disposable hospital period panties. You fear that if you stand up, you might double as a fire hazard and a fashion faux pas. When you ride past the sliding glass doors after the anesthesia wears off, reality sets in. That euphoric, hospital honeymoon stage lingers, but with it come spurts of exhaustion and guilt. Otherwise known as motherhood.

As a mother of two, I don't ask for much. Just some occasional "mommy" time. Time alone. Time to breathe. Through the years, I've taken what I can get—ten minutes in the bathroom post bran flakes here, five minutes at the bank drive-through lane there. The bottom line? I just need some time to vent. To let out my feelings, frustrations, and complain on and on — with no consequences — about every-thing I go through as a mother. In an ideal world, I'd have a girls' night out once a week to get my mental wiggles and giggles out. When I hear what other moms go through, I feel better about myself as a mother. I feel a little less nuts knowing that I'm not alone.

VENTING

4

CRAB DIP AND RUNNING RAFFI

CHEESE: CRAB CHEESE DIP from Marie in Rhode Island

1 (16-ounce) can of crab meat
1 (8-ounce) package of cream cheese
1½ teaspoons of Worcestershire sauce
2 teaspoons of lemon juice
1 clove of garlic, minced
Dash of salt and pepper
¼ cup of light cream
Chopped parsley (to garnish)

Place crab meat in a large mixing bowl. Add cheese, Worcestershire sauce, lemon juice, and other ingredients except parsley. Stir until well blended. Spread in a serving dish. Sprinkle with parsley. Serve with crackers, bagel chips, or tortilla chips.

WHINE: from Mommy Blogger Raffi Darrow of runningbetty.com

The first time I took my first daughter to the doctor was for her one-week checkup. Being as naive as I was, I thought we would arrive at our appointment time, see the doctor for a checkup, and leave. I didn't think about sick kids throwing things off schedule, and I was not yet in the habit of bringing a diaper bag with me everywhere I went.

After sitting in the waiting area for quite a while and finally getting called in the room, my daughter had soaked her diaper. And I didn't have a clean one with me. I asked the nurse for one and she looked at me like I was nuts. I guess I thought they'd have samples around, like they gave out samples of baby formula. When the doctor arrived, they took off the soaked diaper to weigh and measure the baby on one of those white metal scales. The cold metal on the naked skin must have freaked the baby out, and she started peeing everywhere. I did the first thing I could think of, and cupped my hands under her, catching the running urine right in the palms of my hands. I looked up and said, "I guess I'm officially a mom. I let her pee right in my hands and I still want to hug her!"

5

LAYERED DIP AND A LITTLE POTTY SEAT SNAFU

CHEESE: CHEESY LAYERED DIP from Jeanne in Rhode Island

1 (8 ounce) package of softened cream cheese
1 jar of chunky fresh salsa
1 head of iceberg lettuce, shredded
1 large tomato, diced
2 cups of shredded cheddar cheese
1 (6-ounce) can of sliced black olives

Mix cream cheese and salsa until well blended. Spread this mixture at the bottom of casserole dish. Layer on the remaining ingredients in the order listed, topping with the sliced olive.

WHINE: a little potty seat snafu from Perri in Rhode Island

We were living in New York at the time and my husband was traveling quite a bit, and I was home from work. After working full time for most of my life, I had cut back to part time and was home with the girls. Rebecca (my older daughter) had a very active imagination and was playing dress up and pretend all the time. On this particular afternoon she had decided to play princess and had gone into the bathroom and found the potty seat — you know, that crazy little thing that you put on the toilet that prevents the kids from falling into the toilet because their tushies are too small. Rebecca put the potty seat on her head and began prancing around the house, using the potty seat as a crown. It looked cute! She was walking around the downstairs of the house for quite a while before she decided to take it off. The only problem is that when she went to take it off, it was stuck. At first it was very funny and she was not bothered, then it became clear that it was very stuck. I had her sit down on the couch and relax while I tried to pull it off, but she had wedged it on pretty good and it was really stuck. So what does a suburban housewife do in this circumstance when her husband is not around? She calls the local police. About fifteen minutes later, the policeman arrived with a large "snipper" in the possibility that we would have to cut it off her. Rebecca at this time was crying after I had been spending the last few minutes continuing to try and get this thing off her head. Then I thought of something different...lubricant. With the police officer watching, I gooed Vaseline all over the top and crown of her head to try and slip it off. After a few minutes it worked. The potty seat came off her head. The nice police officer smiled and left. How embarrassing.

The funniest thing about this story is that Rebecca re-tells it all the time. Clearly this was a rite of passage.

6

VENTING

CHEESY BEER DIP AND BABY #3

CHEESE: BEER CHEESE DIP from Molly in Massachusetts

> *2 (8-ounce) packages of cream cheese, softened*
> *2 (8-ounce) packages of shredded cheddar cheese*
> *½ teaspoon of garlic powder*
> *½ cup of beer*
> *1 (1-pound) loaf of round bread*

Place cheeses, garlic powder, and beer in a large bowl. Blend using an electric mixer. Remove top of round bread and place to the side. Hollow out the loaf, saving bread pieces. Scoop cream cheese mixture into the hollowed loaf. Use the bread pieces for dipping. Replace sliced-off bread top between servings.

WHINE: from Jane in Boston, Massachusetts

When my older children were six and four, my husband and I thought we had the routine down pretty well—you go here, I'll go there, and we'll meet up later with both kids in tow. Somehow, it all worked out and we always ended up back at our house safe and sound, the children tucked in safely at night. That was until our third child, Daniel, arrived. When Daniel was about six weeks old, we decided to venture out to dinner for the first time as a family of five. So, we piled into the minivan and off we went to the nearby Ground Round for a "pay-what-you-weigh" cheap meal (cheap because only the kids get on the scale, not the adults—thank goodness, since I had just delivered a baby six weeks earlier!). My husband was kind enough to drop us off at the front while he went to park the car. I took "them," meaning the children, into the restaurant and waited to be seated. Within a few minutes, my husband joined us inside the restaurant. As he walked in, I noticed that he was empty handed, while I had one child on each hand. I looked to the floor and all around and still could not find that my husband had brought anything in with him. Finally, after what seemed like an eternity, but was probably only a matter of seconds, I said to him, "Where's Daniel?" to which he responded, "With you." "No, he's not," I said, to which he replied, "Well, you said you were taking 'them' into the restaurant with you while I went to park the car. 'Them' means the children, doesn't it?" I said, "Well, when I said 'them,' I meant the older two, not the baby." He snidely retorted, "Well, excuse me for thinking that when you said 'them,' you meant *all* of our children, since we now have three!" "Oh, my God," I screamed, "while we are standing here arguing, the baby's in the car, in the parking lot, in the dark, all by himself! Go get him!" As we both went red in the face from embarrassment, my husband rushed out to get poor Daniel out of the car! While we continued to wait for a table, I noticed a very pregnant woman holding the hand of a little girl. I said, "Second child on the way?" She responded, "Yes, any day now." I said, "Oh, congratulations, but can I give you a word of advice? Think long and hard before having a third!" What had once been established as a fairly good routine had suddenly turned into chaos, as we both realized that we would be forever outnumbered by our children!

As the years went on, we got better at managing the three of them when we had been so used to having only two. But Daniel always had a tendency to wander off whenever we were at sporting or other events with the other two. So, the proverbial question halfway through the T-ball game or the soccer game or the hockey game was, "Where's Daniel? Has anyone seen Daniel?" It became such a part of my vocabulary and such a natural instinct to ask that question that often times, I would find myself inquiring of Daniel's whereabouts when he was sitting on my lap or I was pushing him in a carriage. People would laugh and say, "He's right in front of you!"

7

VENTING

A TEXAN SAVES THE MILK AND SPREADS THE CREAM CHEESE

CHEESE: TEX-MEX CREAM CHEESE DIP from Lee in Texas

> ½ *pound of ground beef*
> 1 *(8-ounce) package of cream cheese*
> 1 *(16-ounce) jar of thick, fresh salsa*

Brown meat in a skillet and drain off any extra fat. Break ground meat into small chunks. Cut the cream cheese into chunks and put it in a slow cooker sauce pan. Stir in the salsa and meat and put the temperature on low until the cheese melts. Stir occasionally so that the dip does not stick.

Once the dip is melted down and looks like dip, it's ready to serve. Keep it in the slow cooker on a low setting to keep it warm. Serve with tortilla chips.

WHINE: from Claire in Dallas

I'll never forget trying to get the whole breastfeeding thing down after my daughter was born.

Sometimes she'd think she was at the drive-thru, start to nurse, then stop—meanwhile, the milk was still coming, and needless to say, I shot quite a few pillows, chairs, and sofas trying to put her down, cover the gushers, and *save the milk!*

Other times, I'd just be trying to enjoy a hot shower when all of a sudden, "let down," and I don't mean I was bummed because the hot water ran out too fast...I mean virtually spontaneous combustion and "thar she blows"... *save the milk!*

The funniest was my husband sitting in our rocking chair and trying to wipe off this "white stuff" that was on the arm. "What is all this stuff on the chair?" he asked. "Oh, just dried breast milk," I answered casually, slowly watching him turn as white as the milk.

And lastly, but not least by any means, is the wonderful new contraption each breastfeeding mom is introduced to in order to "help" her bottle breast milk, ya know, taking a little of the load off her so someone else can feed the never-sleeping newborn...the breast pump, probably invented by men just to make sure we're not feeling too all-powerful after just having created another human being...just pop these suckers to each breast, turn the machine on, and now you see how Elsie the cow feels, minus the cow stall.

Yes, the melodic hum of the pump pulling and tugging at your already tender nipples that were just hoping for a little respite from the attack only two hours ago.

Aw, the joys of motherhood — and don't even get me started on back fat…that's just cruel and unusual punishment.

8

WHERE DELANEY AND BUFFALO CHICKEN DIP ROAM

CHEESE: BUFFALO CHICKEN DIP from Cecile in Rhode Island

> 2 (10-ounce) cans of chunk chicken, drained
> ¾ cup of red hot sauce
> 2 (8-ounce) packages of cream cheese, softened
> 1 cup of ranch dressing
> 1½ cups of shredded cheddar cheese

Heat chicken and hot sauce thoroughly in a saucepan. Stir in cream cheese and ranch dressing. Cook, stirring, until well blended and warm. Mix in half the cheddar cheese and transfer mixture to a slow cooker. Sprinkle the remaining cheese over top, cover, and cook on low setting until hot up to 40 minutes. Serve with crackers or tortilla chips.

WHINE: from Becca in Massachusetts

A less-than-proud mommy moment occurred when my daughter Delaney was three years old. She was sent to her room for being fresh. Unable to express her frustration, she began trashing her room. Instead of understanding that she was simply acting out, I went to her room and told her she was acting like an animal. Then I proceeded to tell her that I was calling the animal catcher to take her away. She began crying and pleading with me not to call. I disturbingly found some pleasure in this and proceeded to pick up the phone and make a fake call arranging the pickup. After dragging it out a bit longer, I finally caved and called it off.

Now I know this sounds absolutely awful, but this is the point when my patience really started to deteriorate. Sean was just one and Laney three. I was trying to work from home doing real estate, which was very difficult with the two kids needing something every second of the day. I suppose I thought that working from home would be the ideal situation. Instead I found it to be extremely frustrating trying to make calls and sound professional while children were simultaneously yelling, crying, or grabbing at my legs.

Now I was very disappointed with myself regarding the animal catcher tactic I used with Laney, so I thought for sure that I would never use it with Sean. Well, I was wrong. There came a day where I had had it. Sean kept testing, so finally I was desperate and threatened to call the animal catcher to take him away. Expecting the same pitiful reaction I received from Laney, I ended up with a big surprise. Sean picked up his little backpack, opened the door, and went outside to wait for the animal catcher. I watched him from the door and waited, just knowing he would come running back. Nope. He waited at the bottom of the walkway, periodically looking back and waving, but didn't give in. Finally, I had to accept defeat and bring him back in.

9

QUESO DIP, OH, SNAP AGAIN

CHEESE: JACKIE'S TEXAS QUESO DIP

I have shown up at many a party with this queso dip and tortilla chips, and I swear I'm not kidding when I say people literally surround the bowl. They always ask for the recipe. It's embarrassingly easy. But not so embarrassing I couldn't share it with you.

> 1 pound of pasteurized processed cheese (yes, like Velveeta)
> Hot peppers (if you don't like it spicy, forget it)
> 1 (10-ounce) can of diced tomatoes with chilies or 1 8-ounce container of fresh salsa (preferably not with corn or beans.)
> Tortilla chips (I like baked tortilla chips with a hint of lime)

Cut the cheese into small chunks and place on stove. Stir in hot peppers and diced tomatoes or salsa. Cook over low heat until melted. Serve with tortilla chips.

You can also try making traditional queso dip in the Crock-Pot. Follow the above directions, but put the cheese and other ingredients in a Crock-Pot and heat on low until the cheese is melted. Also, the dip can be made on the stove top and then kept warm in the Crock Pot. If you're in a hurry, microwave all the ingredients in a microwave safe dish for 90 seconds or until all the cheese is melted.

WHINE: oh, snap again, from Jackie

Don't get me wrong, I love my children and always wanted to be a mother. When I think back to my childhood days, I played house until I was too old to play house. Starting as a two-year-old, I played mommy to a plastic baby doll. And boy, did that dream of becoming a mother come true, three days shy of my thirtieth birthday. I found myself sitting on an inflatable doughnut, my privates feeling like they had been raked over by a tractor, holding my beautiful firstborn. My son turned out to be a polite and fun-loving child, but during his toddler years, there were times when I thought I couldn't take it anymore. Like any mother, I tried harder, not smarter, forgot about the challenges, and gave birth to a second child. Some say you have kids when you're young because that's when you have the most energy. I say we have kids when we're young because when we're young, we're naive. I'm not a bitter person, I'm actually an optimist. I adore my son and daughter and treasure raising them. But after thirty-one hours of labor and two hours of pushing with my firstborn, and the doctor tell-

ing my husband I may not make it, was it wrong to expect things to fall into place? That somehow, some way,
my firstborn would magically turn out like the babies in
the Pottery Barn catalog? I'd spin him around while my
highlighted hair blows in the wind and he'd do everything
by the book? After months of new-baby bliss, something
happens. The poop, basically, hits the fan. In between the
diaper changes, sleepless nights, and headachy afternoons,
reality sets in. And we snap. Even the most optimistic of us
are transformed into whiny women. But it's not our fault—
we don't mean to be this way. We don't ask for this—it just
happens.

When I look back at the time in my life when I had my
second baby and a three-year-old, fifteen minutes to myself in a barn stall would have sufficed. I didn't realize it
at the time, but all I needed was a little time to myself.
Some women lose themselves when they become mothers. I think this happened to me. We are so exhausted, and
so blinded by sleeplessness; we become mommy martyrs,
determined to do everything for everyone else. We think
that by spending uninterrupted time with our kids, we
will miraculously become better mothers. But this is not
always the case. (Unless you are one of those moms who
gives birth to baby number four without drugs and tills
in the garden a few days later with a calm, sleeping baby
snuggling against your bosom.) I think one of the reasons
women like this have such big families is because their experience from pregnancy to childbirth and beyond is so in-
satiably positive. Good for you if you fall in this category.
You are my hero and pseudofrenemy. I heart you and can't
relate to you at the same time.

I was dealing with an active little boy that happened
to throw tantrums at random while I took care of his new

baby sister. He was the little man of my dreams that never stopped long enough to let me fit in a decent phone conversation. Then there was the laundry, bills, searching for a new "post-second-baby" job, and arranging food to look like I made a decent dinner by the time my husband walked through the door. But there was no "mommy time" to be found. My hands smelled of dried poop, my ass had expanded, I was lonely and sleep deprived. I was in love with my children, but I was losing myself. At times, or actually, every other hour, I reached for spoonfuls of peanut butter to satisfy my pangs. And I actually had a love affair with Nutella for several months. It wasn't until I made some fabulous girlfriends and we bitched to one another without consequence that I started feeling like myself again.

10

TOASTED LOGS WITH WINE JUICE

CHEESE: TOASTED CHEESE LOGS from Janet

2 cups of grated sharp cheddar cheese
1 teaspoon of Worcestershire sauce
1 teaspoon of mustard, plain or spicy
Dash of cayenne pepper
3 tablespoons of cream
Thin slices of bread, crusts removed

Combine cheese, Worcestershire sauce, mustard, cayenne, and cream. Spread on trimmed bread. Roll slices to make "logs." Place on a lightly greased baking sheet and toast in a 350°F oven or under broiler until lightly browned.

WHINE: from Kirsten in Rhode Island

My son's preschool teacher, Miss Rosalyn, pulled me aside one afternoon when I was picking him up from preschool. "If you have a second," she started cautiously, "I wanted to let you know something that Ben shared in class today." (You know that feeling that you get when you are positive that the next thing you are going to hear won't be good? This was one of those times.) She continued, "Umm, well, Ben said that you gave him some wine to drink." (Okay — here we go.) "Well, yes, actually, that's right. I did give him a sip of wine," I replied forced-casually. (Can you hear the pin drop? Can you picture the *big* saucer eyes on this early-childhood educator? You're not even close.) "I see," she said. ("I see," as in, "I am sooooo putting this into your file.") "My husband was having a glass of red wine and Ben asked what it was. I told him it was grape juice for grownups and I asked him if he wanted to try a sip. And he did." And there you have it. I'm Mother of the Year! Now where's the bottle opener?

11

SPINACH DIP AND MODERN-DAY TUPPERWARE PARTIES

CHEESE: REBECA'S FAMOUS SPINACH DIP, by Rebeca, founder of the Average Parent

> 1 small (about 10-ounce) box of frozen chopped spinach, thawed
>
> 1 (about 14-ounce) can of artichoke hearts, sliced
>
> 1 (8-ounce) box of cream cheese
>
> 1 cup of grated Parmesan cheese
>
> ⅓ cup of mayonnaise
>
> ⅓ cup of sour cream
>
> ½ teaspoon of red pepper flakes
>
> ¼ teaspoon of salt

¼ teaspoon of garlic powder

Boil spinach and artichokes in 1 cup of water until tender and drain. (I use the microwave for about 5 minutes.) Discard liquid and squeeze dry in strainer. In a separate bowl, heat cream cheese in microwave for 1 minute or until hot and soft. Then stir in rest of ingredients, along with the spinach and artichokes, and serve hot with crackers, chips, or pita wedges.

WHINE: Jackie's rant on Tupperware parties

As a mom, there are times when you feel the need to roll up in a ball, head for the corner, and hide. (A yoga-inspired technique I wish I'd tried when my kids were four and one.) But you rationalize the situation and realize all you really need is time away with the girls. When my kids were really little, I took the initiative to plan a night out with a group of girlfriends that I hadn't seen in ages. Doing something like this sounds like an easy enough task. But for some reason—I guess the fact that at the time, we were all mothers to toddlers—we couldn't seem to get our acts together. You realize in the midst of planning that, deep down, your attempt will fail. Somehow, something is inevitably going to go wrong. Despite trading twelve e-mails, leaving four voice mails, and having a half-baked conversation with a friend as your youngest child is having a fit in the middle of the produce aisle, something will go awry. It doesn't matter if a husband is finally home from a business trip, because one of your kids is going to get sick. Another girlfriend is going to call and say she's sorry, but she's just too tired, and another will have to cancel because it's just not a good night. Another plan for a girls' night out delayed. You'll try to reschedule two months down the road, but something always comes up. A mysterious elementary-school virus strikes, hitting every household, delaying the planning another three weeks. Then July comes, and we're all away on vacation.

When do mothers actually get together? When one of us hosts a modern-day Tupperware party, selling some swanky line of jewelry, clothing, or toys. Miraculously, our schedules align; we blow out our hair, slap on some mascara, pull on our dressy jeans, and show up with checkbooks in hand. Don't get me wrong. I don't completely detest these parties. I enjoy getting together with girlfriends, but I could do without all the products, price points, and presentations. Is it wrong to want whine and wine time with the girls without having to pay $57 for a pair of plastic earrings I might wear twice? We only have a few minutes to trade "ass-out" hugs and shove down sushi and wine before one woman we barely know starts doing a mini-presentation on products that we don't really need, but buy anyway in hopes that we'll be invited to the next get-together so that we can ultimately squeeze in another twenty minutes of socializing and giggling without the kids.

Deep down, all we want is a little free time to hang out with other moms, but somewhere in our minds, attending these pay-to-stay dates justifies our making special plans to get together without our kids. It's like a carousel of disappointment—our hopes and hairdos teased into a euphoric high but the reality of the situation brings us down again, and around and around it goes. We are left feeling slightly disappointed and exhausted from fake smiling when we've hit our "wall."

After nights like these, I go home and eat a block of cheese the size of a computer speaker, recounting my shameless and unnecessary purchases.

12

CHOPPED BROCCOLI AND VAGINA TALES

CHEESE: HOT BROCCOLI DIP from Rebeca at the Average Parent

My top recipe for this year is Hot Broccoli Dip, which is a variation of a recipe I found through Cabot (the cheese company). It's very similar to spinach dip, with a few differences that can really make it stand out at any party.

1 (10-ounce) package of frozen chopped broccoli

8 ounces of Cabot Seriously Sharp Cheddar, Vintage Choice Cheddar, or other premium extra sharp cheddar, grated

4 ounces of cream cheese

1 cup of parmesan cheese (add more to taste, if desired)

½–1 teaspoon of garlic powder (to taste)

½ teaspoon of crushed red pepper flakes

Place frozen broccoli in microwave-safe bowl; cover loosely with plastic wrap and microwave until hot and tender, about 9 minutes (do not add any water).

Mash broccoli with potato masher until large chunks are gone.

Add cheddar, cream cheese, parmesan cheese, garlic powder, and pepper to bowl. Cover again and microwave just until cheeses are melted, 1 to 2 minutes longer. Stir until smooth. (If mixture seems thin, it will thicken upon cooling.)

Serve with crackers—I prefer Triscuits, but hubby likes Toasteds.

WHINE: vagina tales from Jackie

It happens nearly every time we get together with other couples. After dinner and a few glasses of wine, we women gradually end up three rooms away from our husbands and start swapping birth stories. Men will brag about their college drinking days, and the women will go on and on about giving birth. I know my husband is sick of me sharing my vagina tales, but I pushed two human beings into this world, so I believe that entitles me to have bragging rights for the rest of my life. It's an inevitable topic. Had I done whiskey shots while riding on a roller coaster without puking, maybe I'd brag about that, too. After all, nobody tells you what really happens during childbirth. Sure—there are books, doulas, classes, and birthing coaches. But until you go through it yourself, it's like trying to learn how to drive a car without getting behind the wheel. It's not even close. Sure, my husband and I went through birthing classes together; we watched the films, practiced breathing, and he placed his hands in a bowl of ice for 10 minutes along with me. It hurt like hell and I whined like a baby, but before I knew it, it was over and we were sitting comfortably in a restaurant in downtown Seattle nibbling on pad Thai. Needless to say, I had a tough time delivering my first child. No one told me it would feel like I had been run over by an eighteen-wheeler and would have to wear maxi pads the size of Texas for six weeks. But after it was over, I was in full-blown honeymoon stage, holding this unbelievable child that looked like ET's little brother. I was in love. And I thought we were in the clear, until we brought him home.

13

CHEESE TACOS AND TRUCK-DRIVER TALKIN' MAMAS

CHEESE: CREAM CHEESE TACO DIP from Rebeca from the Average Parent

This recipe is one of my favorite party dishes simply because everybody loves it and it's so incredibly easy to make. Plus, you can store leftovers in the fridge for late-night snacking. Yum!

Here's what you need:

2 (8-ounce) boxes of cream cheese, softened
2 (8-ounce) jars of medium Ortega taco sauce
Shredded lettuce

1 bag of shredded cheddar cheese
1–2 small tomatoes, chopped
1 (4 ounce) can of sliced black olives

Whip cream cheese and taco sauce with an electric mixer until smooth. Spread evenly over a round serving platter. (I like to use disposable pizza pans). Layer with lettuce, cheddar, tomatoes, and olives, and serve with your favorite tortilla chips (we like Tostitos Bite Size Rounds).

WHINE: no truck-driver talkin' mama from Jackie

In our home, I try to use substitute phrases like "For the love of Christmas," "Dang it," "Sugar," "Jinkies," "Mother of Pearl," and "Holy Tamale" to protect my kids from real bad language. I have to resort to these rather lame phrases because I have a tendency to talk like a sailor when I'm among friends. But I'm not an idiot—I know my kids aren't exactly living under a rock. When my son was in kindergarten, he informed me that his private part is called "Peter." That was shocking enough, coming from a five-year-old. In my sister-in-law's house, "stupid" has always been considered a bad word, and I catch flack from all the nieces and nephews when I accidentally spew out the word. When my daughter started talking, she had a difficult time putting *T* and *R* together. Everything *T* or *TH* winds up sounding like *F*. This is not a good thing for a variety of reasons. Every time she sees a truck, my youngest child proudly shouts out the F word, repeatedly, for everyone to hear. And all my substitute phrases, along with my mommy pride, flies out the window. Son of a, holy, for the love of…!

MORE WHINE: from Becca (from Massachusetts), a Mommy Moment on a similar topic

The other day the kids were fighting and calling each other names. They know that "stupid" is one of the words that's not allowed. While trying to rush the kids out the door, I must have slipped and said something was stupid. Laney instantly caught it and said, "Mom, don't say 'stupid.' " I suddenly whipped around like the exorcist and very maturely yelled, *"Stupid, stupid, stupid."* Head bobbing and all. The kids just stopped in their tracks and then started to laugh. So there it was: Mom having a mini-tantrum. Not my prettiest moment.

14

FIGGY CHEESE AND PRIVACY, PLEASE

CHEESE: CHEDDAR CHEESE DIP WITH DRIED FIGS from "the Cheese Impresario," Barrie Lynn, who writes "Cheese Matters"

1½ cups of grated aged Wisconsin cheddar (these cheese-makers sure know how to make cheddar)
1½ cups of sour cream
Salt and pepper as you like it
1 cup of minced dried California figs, Mission (black) or Calimyrna (golden)

Mix all the ingredients except the figs until your dip is the smoothness you like. I enjoy mine a little chunky. Then fold in the minced dried figs. Place in a pretty serving bowl and chill for a couple of hours. Bring your Cheddar Cheese Dip with Dried Figs out of the fridge about ½ hour before you're going to put it out for your guests.

I love this spread on an artisan whole-wheat loaf sliced and very lightly toasted. I use La Brea Bakery's Whole Wheat and Honey Loaf that's available in most grocery stores these days. You can also use this spread on all kinds of burgers to enjoy the sweet/savory flavors.

WHINE: Some privacy, please **from Marie in Maryland, a former mommy blogger**

A few things you give up when becoming a mom: energy, an active social life (or at least one that involves bars and such), blowing loads of money on frivolous things just for you, making a bowl of cereal for dinner and calling it a day, and privacy! My latest invasion from my mini-stalker:

My back hurts, my feet are swollen, it is a lazy Sunday afternoon, Lucy is somewhere playing something quietly, perfect opportunity to grab a book and take a nice, long, hot bath. (Not so much). About ten minutes into my bath, a little monster comes barreling through the door wanting to know what I'm up to. "Ooooo, a bath! I want to play!" Next thing I know I have a mermaid Barbie joining me in the tub and a four-year-old hanging over the side. But apparently that isn't enough...

Lucy: "I'm just going to stick my feet in, okay?" (Climbs up on the side of the tub feet in my water.)

Me: "Umm, okay, I guess." (Continues reading, trying hard to ignore.)

Of course the invasion doesn't stop here. A few pages later Lucy is in her birthday suit and almost finished with the full bath takeover. She looks up and says to me:

"You know, Mom, there really isn't much room in this bath for two people. You would probably be more comfortable reading on the couch downstairs."

Girls' night before kids.

Girls' night after kids.

15

GOAT CHEESE TARTS AND THIRTY-SOMETHING OLD PHARTS

CHEESE: CARAMELIZED ONION AND GOAT CHEESE TARTS from Alice in Georgia

Tarts:

> 1 (about 1 pound) pie or unflavored pizza dough
> Olive oil
> Goat cheese spread:
> 1 (8-ounce) package of goat cheese, softened
> ½ cup of heavy cream

1 tablespoon of lemon juice
Dash of salt and white pepper

Caramelized onions:

2 tablespoons of olive oil
3 large yellow or Spanish onions, thinly sliced
1 clove of garlic, minced
1 teaspoon of salt
1 teaspoon of pepper
1 teaspoon of sugar
2 teaspoons of finely chopped flat-leaf parsley

For the tarts: Preheat oven to 350°F. On a floured surface, roll out pie or pizza dough ⅛-inch thick. Cut dough into 15 (4-inch) circles. Pierce dough randomly with a fork. Brush lightly with olive oil. Bake for 5–7 minutes, until golden brown and crisp. Remove from oven and cool.

For the goat cheese spread: Combine all spread ingredients.

For the caramelized onions: Heat olive oil in a large skillet over low heat. Add onions and cook until translucent. Add garlic, salt, pepper, and sugar; cook for about 10–15 minutes, until onions are dark brown and sweet. Stir in parsley. Remove from heat and cool.

To assemble: Spread some goat cheese mixture over each crust. Spread caramelized onions over goat cheese. Bake for 5–7 minutes. Yields 15 tarts. Serve immediately and enjoy.

WHINE: from Jackie on girls' night out pre- and postkids:

Girls' night out prekids = Go out with friends to a bar, dance, and vent about life until 2 a.m.

Girls' night out postkids = Send out twelve e-mails, make five phone calls over six weeks to organize. Once we've agreed on a date, we finally get together; but one girl calls to cancel because her son is throwing up, and two others are thirty minutes late. Share appetizers and sip two drinks each, tops. We're all home by 9:27 p.m., just in time to catch recorded TV shows. It takes two days of headaches and sleeplessness to get over our tame night out.

Guys' night out prekids = My husband and four friends meet at a bar after work and play pool until 2 a.m.

Guys' night out postkids = One guy sends an e-mail at noon; everyone agrees on a time. Boom, they are out at a bar by 6:30 p.m. the same night and home by 11 p.m., just in time to eat leftovers and watch sports highlights.

16

BROWN SUGAR BRIE AND BOYS VS. GIRLS

CHEESE: BAKED BRIE WITH BROWN SUGAR from Debbie

> *1 sheet of puff pastry*
> *1 (8 ounce) wedge brie, rind removed, and cut into 1-inch*
>   *chunks*
> *Brown sugar*
> *Dried currants*
> *Chopped pecans*

Thaw puff pastry at room temperature for 30 to 45 minutes, then unfold and place in a baking dish. Place chunks of brie evenly down center of pastry. Sprinkle brown sugar, currants, and pecans over brie. Fold sides of pastry up and over cheese mixture and press lightly to seal. Cover with foil and bake at 375°F for about 10 minutes. Remove foil and bake for another 15 minutes.

WHINE: from Jackie, boys vs. girls

Many of us have pondered the question: who is tougher to raise — girls or boys? Having one of each, I can tell you there's no easy way to answer this question. My son was an active baby and toddler, and I never sat down enough to know what day it was let alone act like a normal person, so I always thought, hands down, that boys were the toughest. I had a girl next, and when she was a day old, she found her thumb, so it was like I hit the baby lottery. She hardly ever cried. She was a dream baby, sleeping through the night most nights. That is, until she turned twenty months. Overnight, she became a raging toddler, full of energy and attitude. A nightmare, as my husband recalls — as if the villain that had invaded my son's toddler body moved into hers. He became, almost overnight, this obedient and well-mannered four-and-a-half-year-old, while she became a difficult toddler, getting into everything. And I mean everything.

I'll never forget the infamous "playdates" with the O'Donnell kids. My son Calvin and daughter Sarah played with the O'Donnells' three kids Teddy, Patrick and Meaghan. They are all well-behaved kids, but there was this one incident that gave me *my* answer to this inevitable question. Calvin and the O'Donnell boys are running through the house with Nerf guns. When I ask, "What are you doing, Calvin?" my son yells from the basement, "Just shooting each other, Mom."

Seems like a reasonable answer, so I keep doing the dishes.

When I call to Sarah and Meaghan and ask how they are doing, my daughter responds, "Nothing, Mom." And this makes me worry. So I go upstairs to check on them and they appear to be fine, playing in her room. "We're playing salon."

I'm a sucker, and I smile because I think this is so cute, just as one of the boys barely misses my face with his Nerf gun as I'm on my way down the stairs.

A few minutes go by and I call for the girls again. Meaghan and Sarah come running down the stairs with wet-looking hair. "Mommy, Mommy—we were playing hair salon!"

I catch a glimpse of their hair.

"Sarah, what do you have in your hair?"

"Nothin'."

"What did you put in your hair?" I ask.

"Nothin'. Just play stuff."

"Sarah, tell Mommy what you put in your hair right now!"

I feel her hair and it's slick and sticky, like…glue. I feel a collection of four-letter words emerge. But before a "Mommy, that's a bad word" phrase escapes me, I realize enough damage had been done. The next thing I know, I'm pretending to be the salon owner, washing, drying, and styling their hair, all the while thanking God that the white globs of goo had been successfully removed from their hair.

And so my answer to the question? Girls. Boys may start out as challenging babies and toddlers, but girls become more challenging with age.

I smirk to myself, because this is nothing compared to what I have coming to me when she turns thirteen.

When I see the look on my neighbor's face with teenagers, I realize I have *no* idea what I'm in for when she gets older.

17

HOT-HEADED CHEESE DIP AND NEVADA MAMA

CHEESE: HOT-HEADED CHEESE DIP from Sally

2 cups of shredded mild cheddar cheese
8 ounces of cream cheese, softened
1½ cups of sour cream
½ cup of cooked diced ham
¼ to ⅓ cup of chopped mild green chiles
Finely chopped jalapeno peppers, to taste, optional
⅓ cup of chopped green onions
⅛ teaspoon of Worcestershire sauce
1 (1-pound) round loaf of crusty bread

In a medium bowl, combine cheddar and cream cheese, sour cream, ham, chile peppers, chopped green onions, and Worcestershire sauce. Mix to blend well. Set dip aside.

Cut a thin slice from top of bread loaf; set slice aside. Using a gentle sawing motion, carefully cut vertically to the bottom of the loaf, ½ inch from the edge. Lift out center of loaf; cut into 1-inch cubes and set aside. Fill hollowed bread loaf with the dip; cover with reserved top slice of bread loaf. Wrap the filled loaf well in foil. Bake at 350°F for 1 hour. Serve with reserved bread cubes, crackers, or potato chips.

Makes about 4 cups of dip.

WHINE: from Norah in Nevada

My mom friends and I share stories on Facebook all the time. Here is a sampling of status updates when my son Devan was just a year old.

NORAH: DEVAN IS GOING TO GROW UP THINKING HIS NAME IS "DEVANNO!"

RESPONSE FROM FRIEND: BETTER THAN "ALEX-GOD-DAMN-IT-YOU-DRIVE-ME-CRAZY!"

Bought a carton of fifteen eggs at the store yesterday. What, you didn't know they sell cartons with fifteen eggs in them? They do if you grab a carton of eighteen eggs, your son proceeds to break three while he is playing in the cart, and you're not paying close enough attention.

Being a mom leaves you with all kinds of questions, like "How in the world did the remote get wet?" This morning, Devan is in the bath, I'm next to it with the laptop on my lap. My feet are up on the rim of the tub. I feel Devan pouring water on my leg, so I look up to see him squatting on the edge of the tub, and not pouring water…but peeing on me!! He's not even seventeen months yet…I'm in so much trouble when he hits his teens!!

Devan is in the front room, screaming and crying. He keeps taking my cell phone off the table, then looking at me. I tell him, "No, put it back." He then puts it back, more screaming and crying, and the process repeats…

Key replacement order #245,252—that's what happens when your son plays with the fireproof safe.

Another Devan tale: Devan had dirty hands from breakfast. He already had the chair by the sink, so I stood him on the chair and washed his hands. He so enjoyed playing in the water that I put the stopper in the sink and let the water run for him. I then walk 30 feet to grab something, turn around, and he is standing…in the sink! Soaked! So, I stripped off his pants and shirt, and let him play in the sink.

Jason is teaching Devan how to use the Xbox remote. I can't decide whether this is awesome (father-son bonding, learning something new) or horrible (too young to start playing video games).

18

COTTAGE CHEESE THIGHS AND NACHO DIP

CHEESE: NACHO CHEESE DIP WITH COTTAGE CHEESE
from Casey in Florida

1 (16 ounce) package of cottage cheese
1 (16 ounce) package of low-fat sour cream
Taco seasoning
Shredded lettuceTomato (diced)
Sliced olives
Green onions
1 (4 ounce) package of shredded cheddar cheese
Tortilla chips
Salsa

Mix cottage cheese, taco seasoning, and sour cream until smooth. Spread mixture onto cookie pan (15x10-inches) and top with lettuce, tomatoes, green onions, cheddar cheese and olives. Chill for about 20 minutes before serving. Serve with chips and salsa.

WHINE: cheese thighs from Sam in Massachusetts

I run every week. Unfortunately, I still have cottage cheese thighs. Two of my kids are in school all day, but my youngest is usually within earshot when I start complaining about my non-runner body. I jiggle my thighs and check myself out in front of the mirror before getting in the shower. "Mountain mama," "cheese curd hips," "cottage cheese thighs," you name it, I call myself these things. I try to make sure I say it when Angie's not in the room. The other day, the mailman rang the doorbell while I was out on a run. My daughter answered.

My husband said he came running down the stairs when he heard my daughter say, "My dad's home, but my mom is running because her legs have too much cheese on them."

VENTING # 19

TURKEY CHILI CHEESE AND WHY MY COUCH IS THE COLOR OF CRAP

CHEESE: CREAMY TURKEY CHILI CHEESE DIP from Meghan Lee in San Francisco

1 (8 ounce) brick of cream cheese (can use low fat)
1 (15 ounce) can of turkey chili without beans
Hot sauce

In a saucepan on the stove top, drop in the cream cheese and break it up so it starts to melt. Then add in the can of chili and mix the two together until they blend. I then add hot sauce (Tapatio or Cholula is the best) to your liking—I add a lot (4 teaspoons) to give the dip a good kick.

Dip with tortilla chips and be prepared to see it go quickly!

WHINE: why my couch is the color of crap, from Jackie

When our son was two, we glanced around our home and realized our post college, slipcovered couch was losing its eclectic charm. So, after procrastinating for several months, we finally went out and bought a grown-up sofa with white, yellow, and blue cotton stripes. Mind you, my mother, grandmother, aunts, mother-in-law, sisters-in-law, cousin, and just about every female in my life tried talking me out of buying it. But I liked it, and, what can I say, we were sold.

Two weeks later, I realized why all the women in my family—even those 1,200 miles away—were on my case. If someone told me they were coming over for a short visit, I'd look at my couch and panic. The cushions were caved in, turning a sorry shade, and always had specks of pink and brown all over them. (Some from nights when I'd fall asleep eating a chocolate bunny, and some from other brownish-tinted unmentionables.) I'd have to zip down the cushions individually, wash them, dry them, and put the shrunken, wrinkly versions back on. Meantime, our son had just started his fascination with rocks, or as he called them, dinosaur eggs. Dinosaur eggs? Every rock, stone, mud pile, and shell found by my son qualified as a dinosaur egg. Dinosaur eggs and juice were two of the many reasons this couch is now in the basement masked by the same slipcover that was covering our old "early marriage" couch. And why our once glass-covered, white-wood coffee table is no longer covered in glass. Today, I have two leather couches the color of crap, or, as most would say, a lovely shade of espresso. And they are my new best friends. They hide everything. I may not know what's in between the cushions every week, and this helps with my perpetual denial. But now, when someone calls to let me know they're stopping by, I look at my two leathered friends and smile.

20

CHEESY BURGER DIP AND REFLECTIONS ON RUST-OLEUM

CHEESE: CHEESY BURGER DIP from Jackie

1½ pounds of ground hamburger
1½ pounds of hot sausage
1 (10.5 ounce) can of cream of mushroom soup
1 (2 pound) box of processed cheese (like Velveeta)
1 (16 ounce) container of fresh hot salsa

Cook hamburger and hot sausage in skillet on medium-high heat. Drain and keep meat in skillet. Add soup, cheese, and salsa, and cook on stove top on low until cheese is melted. This recipe serves about a dozen people.

WHINE: reflections on Rust-Oleum from Jackie

My son is all grown up and potty trained, has been for many years. But the words "boy" and "urinate" have taken on an entirely new meaning in our home through the years. Now my new concerns are "aim" and "stain."

Here's my post-potty-trained dilemma: Should I nag my son for missing the bowl when he pees, hence corroding the metal base board next to the toilet? Or should I hold my breath and blame the contractor who put a white metal heating system next to the commode?

Every time he goes to the downstairs bathroom, which is conveniently and inconveniently located next to the kitchen, I cringe and giggle simultaneously. He's still my good boy. But he is a boy. And I know he's going to miss. I can sense it. Like a crazed mom, as soon as he leaves the bathroom, I rush in and spray cleaner wherever he's missed. We repaint that particular bathroom with Rust-Oleum every year. Not seeing the yellow streaks on the base board for even a few days helps keep his mother sane.

VENTING

21

HOT BACON DIP AND THE HORRORS OF SHOPPING WITH KIDS

CHEESE: Hot Bacon Dip from Diana

1 (8 ounce) container of sour cream
8 ounces of mayonnaise
1 (7 ounce) can of chipotle peppers
1 ounce real bacon pieces (bacon bits not recommended)
1 cup of shredded cheddar cheese

Chop up peppers. Mix peppers with sour cream and mayonnaise. Fold in cheddar cheese and bacon. Refrigerate for two hours and serve with tortilla chips.

WHINE: the horrors of shopping with kids from Jackie

I could dedicate an entire book to venting about shopping with my children. Whether it involves spitting, yelling, running, chasing, timeouts, side swiping, spilling, pushing, laughing, crying, screaming, burping, or accidental stealing, I've been through it all.

I must say I probably sound like a wimp to even begin to complain about shopping with one child. Now that I have two kids, I think that qualifies for something. But when you have friends with three, four, even five kids, you tend to stop yourself before even volunteering any information on this topic, regardless of how much you need to vent. Maybe that's why our grandmothers shopped after their husbands came home from work? My neighbor had four children and looked at me with that knowing look when I asked her how she shops with her kids. "I try to avoid it at all costs." It doesn't matter how big your little ones are or how many kids you have, bringing them to the store is a lot like throwing up. You never want to do it, but when the time comes, you realize you have no choice – and you know you'll feel so much better when it's over. I used to put my kids into those obnoxiously wide mini-van-style kiddie shopping carts so they could pretend to drive while I shopped. This sounds all nifty until you go shopping in aisles that are so narrow, you'll get side-swiped if you hold a box of cereal the wrong way. When shopping with kids, I collect as many edible products as possible while keeping their little fingers, arms and legs inside the cart and simultaneously crossing items off my list as fast as I can. I don't mind substituting items like butter for cream cheese as long as I can get through it without hurting anyone. I'll sort it out and deal with the extra cheese on my ass after they hit college. I have this annoying tendency to whisper yell to my children at the store. I try to use this tactic to get them to stop doing whatever it is they're doing that isn't appropriate using my "inside voice." This works for about 5 minutes. "No," I whisper-yell. "Stay in the cart." "Get back in the cart." "Watch your foot." "Watch your hand." "No." "Now put that down." "Stop touching your sister." "Don't put that in your mouth." "Use your manners." "Get back here this instant." "Stop yelling." "What did you just say?" I say, fake smiling and nodding at others. "Get back here. Stop doing that. Put that down!" At this point, my voice is getting louder and people are starting to stare. "Get away from that shelf, you're in someone's way, get back in the cart."

At this point, you should be leaving the store, as my parenting books suggest. But when I'm with my kids, my inner idiot tends to shine. And I get stubborn and give in. After all, I only have three items left and I'm too far along to start from scratch. So I decide, since I already have an audience, that it's OK to talk in a normal tone. This method of mothering, not surprisingly, isn't very effective. It gives off these "So, you're the crazy lady with kids" looks. By the time I get in my car, I've crossed off my shopping list along with every "Don't" tip imaginable. But I get by. And I surprise myself at times. During one particular shopping trip when my kids were toddlers - I got through the automatic doors with smiling children in tow, swept past the produce aisle, grabbed the greenest bunch of bananas, lettuce and over-ripe strawberries, and upon reaching the bakery, nearly crashed into an elderly store clerk, knocked down a cake display and apologized to three customers as I flew past the narrow aisles. Thankfully, I don't frequent this store any more. Unless I'm alone. Without my two kids, I pass for normal. I once blocked the exit doorway for a full minute when my then two-year-old refused to move out of the way. By the time I picked her up and put her back in the cart, she was crying so hard, I thought someone was going to call the local authorities.

Some other unforgettable shopping trips:

We ventured out one day to get my son's haircut. My daughter was a week away from being completely potty trained. Although I asked her that predictable question before we left, the minute we walked into the salon, I asked her again. "Honey, do you have to go to the bathroom?" She said "No, I OK." I prayed she was telling the truth, to make up for the fact that I was being foolish by not putting on a pull-up before leaving the house. This is what happens when I don't get enough sleep. Five minutes later, we walk over to the shampoo station and there, in front of three hair stylists, my daughter squats (without getting her floral dress wet, mind you) and pees all over the floor. I was mortified. I would have left at that moment had the lady not been so understanding, helping me wipe up the wet mess before finishing my son's haircut.

While shopping in Pottery Barn for Kids, my pre-potty-trained son was playing with an electronic dinosaur display when I noticed an odor that could melt the plaid off of a pillow sham. I knew it was him because he was pretending to be distracted when I asked him if he went potty. All he wanted to do was tinker with the talking T-Rex, which I have to admit, was pretty awesome. He proceeded to have a tantrum when I told him we had to leave (so I could change him). I walked out – humiliated, smelling of feces, with a screaming toddler flailing from my hip.

Target: My daughter was having a field day with all the beeping baby toys in the toddler aisle one day. She started screaming when I told her it was time to go. I put one of the toys in the cart so she could play with it and promptly removed it from the shopping cart when we got to the check-out line. Rather than dealing with a toddler screaming inside the store, I experienced it 10 times worse in the parking lot after she realized the toy was not coming home with us.

Becca's shopping experience: For some reason the women that work at this fabric store are always grumpy and sometimes rude. I was going in with my then 5 year old daughter Laney. I wanted to make sure she behaved so I told her about the grumpy women. Big mistake! Throughout the entire store she kept asking me about the grumpy women. "Why are they grumpy?" she asked. "Where are they?" "Is that one of them?" When we were checking out, Laney looks at the cashier and loudly asked if she was the grumpy lady. I of course was horrified and tried changing the subject.

Mom today.   In the 1950's.

22

EASY RANCH DIP AND THE PAINS AND PLEASURES OF PLAYDATES

CHEESE: Easy Ranch Dip from Jeannette in Florida

1 package of ranch salad dressing mix
2 packages (8 ounce) cream cheese, softened
1/3 cup beer or nonalcoholic beer
2 cups (8 ounces) shredded cheddar cheese
1 Bag of Pretzels

Mix cream cheese, beer and dressing in a bowl until smooth. Stir in cheddar cheese. Serve with pretzels.

WHINE: the pains and pleasures of playdates from Jackie

In the 1950's and 1960's, I don't know how mothers did it. They could chase after six kids while fixing a five-course meal wearing four inch heels. Decades later, I'm breaking a sweat after reheating dinosaur chicken nuggets and playing Wii in ballet flats. I think the difference lies in the way kids played back then. "Go play outside," is all mother had to say, and off we went. Today, it's all about play dates, or scheduled get-togethers with other kids, as my husband likes to call them. Back then, kids would come home from school and play on their own, giving moms plenty of time to do all the housework without losing their patience. When I was a kid, I was out of the house so often, my parents didn't expect me to be home until the street lights came on. My best friend and I tried to run away when we were 10 years old, but we only got a few miles away on our bikes and no one noticed until we were gone for more than six hours. Six hours? I can't go to the bathroom for six minutes without my daughter hunting me down. If my kids don't have scheduled playdates every week, they start looking like they need anti-depressants.

There are times when I'll host six or seven kids at my house for a mega playdate. Some moms think I'm a mad woman. The secret to a successful get together lies in how well the kids get along. We found the perfect chemistry with three kids – siblings - who lived about a half mile away from us. The boys would never complain about being bored – they were always finding things to do. And my daughter and their little sister got along so well, they would end up in pink tutus, wheeling baby doll strollers up and down our driveway. There is a purpose to my multi-dimensional playdate madness. When successful, something about them brings out the never-before-seen side of me as a mother.

Any non-domestic side of my work-from-home-stay-at-home mom role fades away, and I'm multi-tasking like a Martha wanna-be. I watch them play while whipping up homemade chili and folding laundry. I check on the kids, play a game or two of tag, and beam with pride at how they are using their imagination, getting fresh air and not sitting in front of the television. In my mind, as I'm folding my daughter's socks, I've become the Kool-Aid mom I always wanted to be. The kids are playing. Dinner will be done in an hour. And I actually made something homemade that doesn't taste like hay stew.

The kids once played outside on a beautiful sunny September day for four hours. Ten minutes before their mom comes to pick them up during this particular play date, they rush in from the backyard, complaining that they are too tired and cold. I tried pleading with them to hang on just a few more minutes, scrambling to find their jackets and a board game. I'm pulling out foam poster board and pipe cleaners when the younger boy starts wailing, grabs another packet of fruit snacks, runs down to our basement and turns on the TV. I cave in, and before another adult human can observe my playdate-hosting abilities, the wheels come off. All five kids are zoned out in front of our basement television watching non-age-appropriate cartoons snacking on stale candy bars when their mom pulls into the driveway.

23

UNHOLY GUACAMOLE AND LESSON LEARNED

CHEESE: Unholy Guacamole from Sue

> 3 avocados (peeled, pitted and diced)
> 1 tablespoon of sour cream
> (3 ounce) packages cream cheese, softened
> tablespoon salsa
> pinch salt
> pinch ground black pepper
> 1 dash garlic salt
> dash onion powder

Mix avocados, cream cheese, sour cream and salsa together in a small bowl. In another bowl, mix salt, pepper, garlic salt and onion powder. Stir ingredients into the avocado mixture. Cover and chill in the refrigerator for 30 minutes. Serve with tortilla chips.

WHINE: lesson learned in air conditioning from Jackie

All school year, we look forward to the summer. The days when we can take the kids to the beach, park, pool club and enjoy hours in the sun as a family. A couple summers ago, by the end of May, I land a new pr project, and the main event is in July, smack in the middle of my kids' summer vacation. I try to stay up late to tackle work so we can do stuff together during the day. Two days into their vacation, my son wakes up, blasts the portable AC unit, wraps himself in a comforter, plays Xbox without permission, and complains that it's too hot to go outside. I turn off my cell phone, slather my kids with SPF 50, and drag them to the pool, where they sit on the edge for 30 minutes complaining that the pool water is too cold. Fifteen minutes later, it starts thundering. The next day, I take them to the park where it's 102 degrees in the shade, and the carousel that opens only in the summer is closed until the following day. We throw the football for 15 minutes, nearly giving me and the kids heat stroke. Lesson learned. Maybe my son had the right idea all along. We would all have been better off hiding under the covers.

If you have a whine or recipe you'd like to share, please write me today at **jackie@ventingsessions.com** or visit my blog at **www.ventingsessions.com.**

ABOUT THE AUTHOR:

Jackie Hennessey is a mom who understands what other mothers go through. She has worked full-time, part-time, and been a stay-at-home mom. She earned a BA in journalism from Texas A&M University and received the "Best Aggie-Life writer" award from the university newspaper. She has more than seventeen years of national experience in public relations and journalism and is currently a PR consultant and blogger in Barrington, Rhode Island. She serves on the Steering Committee for Dress for Success Rhode Island, volunteers at her kids' schools, and enjoys networking with women and venting with other moms every chance she gets: at the monkey bars, book groups, in line at the grocery store, and during those treasured girls' nights. For more information, visit www.ventingsessions.com.